BEN COLAROSSI

360 POUNDS OF
Tears

Copyright © 2022 by Ben Colarossi

All rights reserved. This book or any portion thereof may not be reproduced or transmitted in any form or manner, electronic or mechanical, including photocopying, recording, or by any information storage or retrieval system, without the express written permission of the copyright owner except for the use of brief quotations in a book review or other noncommercial uses permitted by copyright law.

Printed in the United States of America
Library of Congress Control Number: 2022918344
ISBN: Softcover 979-8-88622-618-8
Hardback 979-8-88622-840-3
e-Book 979-8-88622-619-5
Republished by: PageTurner Press and Media LLC
Publication Date: 12/07/2022

To order copies of this book, contact:
PageTurner Press and Media
Phone: 1-888-447-9651
info@pageturner.us
www.pageturner.us

Contents

The Most Beautiful 1
The Love of You 2
Thief of Innocence 4
Behold the Wickedness 5
There Be Tight 6
Peep Out Her Eyes 7
Sounds of Sorry, Not of Command 8
Brick of Time 10
Touch 11
My Heart Cries Sunset Bound 12
Horns of Man's Heart 13
A Touch of Love 15
Fuck Off 16
My Heart 17
A Mother's Love 19
I've Died, Do You Know Me 21
I Like You 23
See Me 24
I Don't Love 25
I Shout Out 26
Tears of My Heart 28
Happiness Knocking On My Door 30
I Cry So Deeply 32
Oh, Woman 34
Heart Dreams of Life 35
The Memory of Love 36
A Girl 38
Christ of Mine 39
The Clouds of Angels 41

Is It You	42
L	43
Why Love	45
My True Self	47
Full-Sized Render	48
Kristel Heart	49
The Lift	50
Kindness upon Thee	51
Forgiveness	52
Loneliness	54

The Most Beautiful

Beautiful is the grace of elegance

Beautiful is a gentleness of the quiet word unspoken

Beautiful is a shyness that warms you

Beautiful is a passing presence that lingers

Beautiful is an invisible gift that touches your heart

Beautiful is an angelic smile that is forever love

I love you so, my beautiful

Benj 4/11/14

The Love of You

Hidden in the darkness of a cave
Hidden deep
A soul full of love, chained
Squinting out into rays of sunlight

Year of not knowing the light
Not feeling the warmth
Always searching

The Love of You

Rushing into my life
As the joy and beauty of a sunrise
Coming up over the horizon
Tickling my soul with hope and anticipation

The Love of You

Showing me what I didn't know
Penetrating the darkness of the cave
Ending my defenses

The Love of You

Has circled my soul
Has opened my heart,
to the light of love

The Love of You

Strong, vulnerable, a look fills my heart

A smile,
Breathing life into my mind

The Love of You

Your love has released me
Showing me the way into the light
I am the man you see
Filled with love
Strong, standing beside you
Holding hands walking through this life together

The Love of You

<u>Benj 2/14/14</u>

Thief of Innocence

Your wicked heart
Beholds your fathers sin
Evil blood runs through your veins
Angels of hate run an armory of frozen stones
To be dammed soon to thee
Father's truth destroyed your heart
Let go,
Embrace the hole in your heart
You were in the depths of hell as a child
Trapped sweetness
Burns the flesh of men
Behold your father's sin
For this will be dammed in the depths of hell
For a life of self-ego and fear
Will be forever among the glory of dark
angels whispering in your ear
Vomit it all out, for the one who loves you is waiting
Safe in the wings of a man's heart of glory
Riding beside him
Your Free!

Benj 5/10/15 11:47 am

Behold the Wickedness

Understand thy heart,
It's a man's revenge of hurt
As I said—
Be what you told of us
We conquer love and hurt
Be slaves to the heads of time
In the course of my love to thee
I hate thy heart
For the hell of wickedness
The devil's weave of deceit
inspire pain and hurt
Oh, the children are born of innocence
A man's tale; his wicked tongue
Changes innocence to fear
Be a sound of words in the seed of thy soul
Oh, wickedness—
Be gone; free us, of your hold
Be the springs of your waters, rays of your white light
Be gone, devil's tongue,
Let it be nailed to the wall—
Breathe in the life you love

Benj 10:20 am 3/13/15

There Be Tight

There be tight upon thee—
Among them believe this
Come upon thee
Believe thou promise
All aboard!

Love of a world of skeletons
Fire of lies

Oh, death of kindness and sorrow
Enter my soul
Grab out the witches of time!

I am the first, the only,
Conquer these forces of will
Come upon thee, let there be peace

Crying out of shame—I love you!
Oh Lord, penetrate my heart
Forgive me
Strengthen me

Benj 10:30 pm 2/13/15

Peep Out Her Eyes

Sound of her lips is like the early morning bird's chirping

As you lift yourself out of bed
They sing into your heart

Breathtaking

She brings you warm thoughts
Every time she smiles

Still young

And very innocent, she is—
But her innocence,
Will carry with her for a lifetime

<u>Benj 8:15 am 1992</u>

Sounds of Sorry, Not of Command

Sounds of sorry not of command
Thy wish is to destroy of nature's gloom

Yonder the clouds weep
As winter falls along icy drips of dew falling gently off the leaf

Grizzly paws of doom linger upon the banks of life

Let there be a shadow on thee that plagues
Centuries of rivers of unpurified souls

For thee is the power and ingestion of a time of
Happiness, that forever is gone

Sounds of sorry, not a command
Thou wish to pluck one's hair one at a time,
To feel the pain of an ocean-salted water

Forever is the light deep in the center of darkness
That was closed in the depths of a well
That was the water of life
But now is a hollow, cracked, dry clay bottom

For you are the life of a seed that has had hope
Thy journey is of hell's command of truth

Sounds of sorry, not a command

For death is the search of life now and forever,
But forever out of reach

How sad we search and search commands of life

Die we shall in this vast unknown of the sorry of life

<u>Benj 12/20/14 8:11 am</u>

Brick of Time

Be the fountain of the world of jovial
Be the past of a God-scented burial
A clove core of belief
For there is a story told—
Of man's love
Yes, this is so
Be there in the midst of time—
God, free my heart
It has been told the brick of time is an illusion of a mind's eye
Be there, allow thy will of happiness—
Oh, God of thy earth
The stars twinkle in thou presence
The vast belief of a world of love—
Let the wicked be still
And the heart be of wine
Flowing of the rivers of time
Thank you! Thank you!
Thank you!

Benj 6:14 am 2/28/15

Touch

Touch
It generates deep in the soul
Touch
It moves men to tears
Touch
It glues hope to life
Touch
Surrounds us,
It engulfs us,
It speaks to us,
Touch
Breathes air into our soul
Touch
—Ah, my friend
Here you are-
And where have you been?
I've longed for you, so much!
You hide on me from time to time-
I long to see you
I cry out your name at night
As my dreams come,
You slither along my body
Gently loving every soul of my being
Oh how I miss you-
I breathe you in
Touch

Benj 3/17/07

My Heart Cries Sunset Bound

My heart cries for you
The taste of your soul—
The look of your eyes
Oh, Lord, release the pain of love
The deepness flows with tears
Longing to hold you, to make love to you
A starer, a glance of your eyes
How I miss thee
My heart wrenches with anger
Only to be softened with the memory of your love—
I scream to thee, stop, stop this pain of regret I love thee,
I love thee,
I'm swallowed up at the river's bottom—
God bring her back to me
Empty my tears
Heal my heart
Forgive me the pain is overwhelming—
I love you so much
Where are those two children—
Who danced with happiness holding hands…
Sunset bound

<u>Benj 4/23/15</u>

Horns of Man's Heart

There are horns revealed
Of the beast who suffers through the agony of men
For it's told angels fear such wrath
Oh Michael, open up the skies
The grunge of darkness
The hatred in thy heart
Cries of love turned into passion of a steel heart
Only men understand
For a woman, high sensitivity, the maker of our existence
Fails the heart of men
Destroy the boy child by her own fears
The juice of your loins
Killer of man's walk of love
Let you suffer of pain
With all you have diseased with your need to be loved
Destroyer of hearts
Destroyer of hope

Destroyer of the sensitivity
For yours is the bosom filled with the nectar of milk
Poisoned of a time
Not a revenge but a passing negative—
Of the loins of generations past
The pain of hurt
Soften thy heart of forgiveness
For I cry out to thee
Goodness or evil my the heavens open up—
Of a tortured, tortured soul and give thy peace
Crying
Crying
Crying

<u>Benj 9:40 am 5/17/15</u>

A Touch of Love

Anticipation
For the brief moment of love—
Shaving, showering, washing-
Anticipating
Her hand loving me
Fear, will she like my body?
Will she go somewhere else in her head—
as she briefly loves me?
That touch, that love
For the brief time my soul and my body cries out!
Hearing her voice,
How gentle is her soul,
Her laughter—soothes my mind
Anticipation
Will I walk away empty for that brief time—
Knowing there is someone else—
Desperately needing that touch
I walk through this life crying inside, looking
Please love me, please accept me, please touch me
Maybe this time she will love me—
Anticipation
Yes— Touch— Yes
No— NEXT!

<u>Benj 1995</u>

Fuck Off

The walls of your blinded hate
Into the skies of your dignity;
Beyond the covers of warmth, for all to see—
The blinded eye of hate, a man's hourglass of sand,
Dripping away—
The gardens of light and mountains
Form the history of this flower's bloom—
Anger exceeds the dreadful abundance
—Of life's black sludge
Deep in your soul screams...
Fuck off—Fuck off!
Memories of hurt and pain—
Life is fleeting by a tortured seed of unhappiness
I scream—screaming!
Love me! Hold me forever in time!
Missing you—
The stars of grace look upon thee
And they twinkle and cry as I try to hold you,
And wisdom of the dead cries tears of your tortured soul
Oh, mother of time - I miss you, I miss you!
So fuck off, fuck off, fuck off—
Fuck off!

Benj 8:34 am 7/1815

My Heart

My heart is so raw
My heart is so raw
The loss of the vision of love that was deep in my soul
Memories of a past life
That linger, that linger with desire
Wanting deep in an epic whirlpool
Of an ocean crying out for love
For the path of darkness screams from an empty well
SCREAMS from an empty well inside me!
Yearning, hoping, reaching out for the light of love
For love is a caretaker of a man and a woman's heart
God's spirit surrounds and engulfs us
Breathe in the light; and breathe in this love
Children playing
Holding hands walking aimlessly
Feeling each other's energy of laughter and love
Eyes dancing among each other;
Playing, running, no fear, no hurt-
Beyond the hurt, a smile, a glance
Reassurance that they are loved
For we all are children
Wanting form the moment we are born into this life
To be loved

Comfort of a belly, of a womb, of a mother's love,
Springing out, crying!
Being placed on the breast of life and comforted
Eyes wide open
Wondering, but needing the comfort of love

For life is all consumed in love
For God's word come to me and I will love you;
Why it's so simple-
Yet we fill ourselves with so much life's awkwardness
Leaving us empty

For I love you
My heart is still broken and sad-
And I know in this universe God can fill that hole
But I am grateful for knowing love for
the brief moment in time...

I'll always love you

<u>Benj May 2015</u>

A Mother's Love

The light of a match quickly blown out
A child's curiosity
Momma's there to teach

A Mother's Love
The moment of sunrise
An inherent love
To gather and surround her children

A Mother's Love
Her husband
Standing beside him-
Invisible whispers

A Mother's Love
Prepare their minds
For the battle and joys of life
Nudging, hugging them along the way

A Mother's Love
She is the core
Giver of life
God has so blessed

A Mother's Love
Worry is a gift
That never settles or compromises
Constant vigilance

A Mother's Love
Popularity is not always
A taste of sugar-
Necessity

A Mother's Love
Popularity is not always
A taste of sugar-
Necessity

A Mother's Love
Her word, her life
Passed on
A mind's eye echoed
In her children

<u>**Benj 3/14/14**</u>

I've Died, Do You Know Me

I've died, do you know me
Were you there when I worried so much
about... will you love?
If I say this or say that-

I've died, do you know me
Were you there when my mommy died at five
All alone in the closet
With my right hand over my ear saying,
"It will be okay, it will be okay,
It will be okay"

I've died, do you know me
Were you there when I sat alone and
Stuffed my face
With food

I've died, do you know me
Were you there when I woke up
Thinking the best day was when I was sleeping

I've died, do you know me
Were you there when I did anything to be touched
Just to be touched,
Just to be loved

I've died, do you know me
Where were you-
When I was being molested at the age thirteen
A scared boy I was

I've died, do you know me
Were you there-
When I abused myself with self-hatred
Calling myself "you fat fuck!"

I've died, do you know
Yes, God! You were there always
Whispering in my ear,
"Ben, I Love you"
"Ben, I love you"
"Ben, I love you"

Benj 3/14/07

I Like You

From the first moment I saw you
Your smile swept across your face
A glance of shyness
You eyes danced and sparkled
There is a warmth and radiance about you
And there is never enough time to spend with you
But . . .
I Like You
You whisk me into your chair and your hands go to work
Once again I am with you gazing into your beautiful eyes
And experiencing your gracefulness
Silently I ponder . . .
How can I entice her . . .
I enjoy being with her so . . . my shyness overwhelms me
It quiets me . . .But . . .
I Like You
Once again the time has come
Always too soon for me to leave
The words I've longed to say
Now are written upon this page
I Like You

Benj 1991

See Me

The little taste of a woman
Those who follow—
Beaten down among the paths of her ego and fear—
There's the gain of power from her loin juices
A tightened flow of water to be quenched,
To choke hold your emotions

To fill your dreams—
To forever leave you abandoned and fluff you off,
As a piece of shit trickles out of your ass—
Her love engulfs you,

Poisons you—
She is gone and laughs at your existence
Not care of your heart
Of your pain
Of your life
For she is the devil's spawn!

Benj 3:20 pm 4/14/15

I Don't Love

I don't love 'til I look in your eyes
I don't love 'til I see your nose crinkle
I don't love 'til I kiss your sweet lips
I don't love 'til I hold you in my arms
In my arms
In my arms
When I kissed you, my lips wanted more
But I can't have you
My heart is crying
My heart is breaking
I don't love
But in your eyes I see, my little girl
My little boy-
Growing inside of you
I don't love
I don't love
Only when I'm with you
I know love
I need your love

Benj 6:30 pm 10/12/06

I Shout Out

Eat the flesh of a man's creation—
Evil destroys a man's heart
The heart is a soul that reaches out for love
And loves this life that is strange
Bad land of a memory that does not exit
For death will come
Life is of moments
Flashes of memories -

We destroy the lineage of time
While times is God's playground,
Death comes and we never know why
The biblical time-
Preaches of this man
Who became of this Earth?
And yet we are to follow

To believe,
To have faith, guilt, and
Shame, that goes along with it-
If you don't believe,
Evil's presence prevails in this life!

It shadows over a man's heart
At times it's easy to be within the fire of rage,
For love is shrouded by the sickness of anger
Fire of an ocean breeze surrenders your soul-
It fills you with love

Darkness of fear floods the light
I fall to my knees
I shout out!

<u>Benj 6:23 am 4/19/15</u>

Tears of My Heart

My eyes fill up with tears
For it's been told in the depth of ones heart

Multiply in the Heart of all walking on this earth
In search of what is beyond

The clouds
Cry and reach in-

The quiet
Fear embraces you
and pours out

I Am, I Am
A man of love

In a whirlpool
of tears taking me under

Reach for me -oh
Heaven

Pull me from this depth
Of pain and degeneration
Of thy self

Years of darkness
Of hell reaching in and torching my mind
Feeding me lies
and vomit of spew
Destroying this vessel
of love

In the light is this love
That shines in me for all to see

For let that light of love
Engulf myself and radiate the truth

My eyes fill up with tears
And the joy of love fills me
And I believe
This is so, this is in me!

<u>Benj 6:10 pm 4/16/16</u>

Happiness Knocking On My Door

Forever, it eludes me
For the memory of time,
Vision of happiness upon the world
It fills me with so much joy

Strawberry red lips linger sweetness of wanting more
I miss you so my love
Please see me

For it is this love, from my heart
That engulfs our happiness

Blessing of a seed
Soft in the womb
This is to be forever
Longing since time has began

Sexiness of this life
Sneaking out
In the freedom of the night

Sweet kisses my love
Hold me close and just love me
Hold my heart

My love
Knock and I will answer
Forever is ours to keep

Cry together in each other's arms
And wipe the tears of sadness

For our love has finally
Found us!

<u>Benj 4:51 am 3/22/16</u>

I Cry So Deeply

I cry so deeply
For love

I cry so deeply
For touch

I cry so deeply
For the sound, a whisper-
I love you

I cry so deeply
For her touch

I cry so deeply
For her to need me

I cry so deeply
For her mouth to kiss me softly-
I love you

I cry so deeply
Watch her sleep, whisper
I love you

I cry so deeply
Waiting for her love

I cry so deeply
Longing for her eyes to
Sparkle when she sees me

I cry so deeply
To hold her, she is safe in my arms

I cry so deeply
Seeing my
Child in her eyes

I cry so deeply
Come to me I will fill
You with love

I cry so deeply
I will not waiver
I'm your Rock

Cry deeply
In my heart, my soul
Walk with me
Side by side
In this life

We cry deeply
With love in our
Hearts together

<u>Benj 8:54 pm 3/6/16</u>

Oh, Woman

Oh, woman

You giveth birth

Protected we shall shield thee with might—

For it's she who creates the grace of time

Hug us

The milk of nectar

A baby's embrace of flowing engulfment

Oh, woman—

Of time we bow upon our knees

I will be the white knight of strength to thee

Benj 4:43 am 2/25/15

Heart Dreams of Life

To fold inside of you
To hold tenderly someone's heart
To kiss . . . and love . . . and gaze into each other's eyes
For god has blessed and brought us together
To hold life
Its precious moments of time fleeting by
How I want to love thee - How I want to hold thee
Oh god of the Highest - Angels comes down upon me . . .
And float forever
The love that I am seeking
For it is in a child's eyes that we meet and our souls entangle
For Love is the only thing in life that we
embrace, that we hunger for -
The kindness . . . the partnership . . . the holding of hand . . .
Holding each other, oh so tight . . . crying
inside and loving each other!
O'lord bring this beautiful loving woman to me
I thank you, I'm grateful to thee
For this life is such a vast entity of mystery
The beauty of the sun, sets and rises
Thank you god for this moment
For I am lonely . . .
And I know I'm not alone because you're with me all the time
But I ask you to bring me the woman my heart desires

And more importantly the life of love
our eternal heart desires
For Love is only the way

Benj 9/6/15 6 am

The Memory of Love

It hurts to be loved
Then let go

The memory
Deep in the shadows

The black and white

The in between

The anger and hatred
Of being forgotten

To feel completed
And tossed aside

The sweet bitterness of a fool
To be mocked of this love

The revenge lingers on you lips
The understanding of a man's crying heart
Released with the fire of a dragon
Melts the faces of those who dared to look that way

All consumed

For man is burned into ashes
Not crying but slapped by even a thought of love lost

For the little boy who cries
is swooped up in arms
of love

For this love is a memory
That is as sweet as a child

A mans cry
Deafening and placed
In a prison corner

Womb position

Not wanting of this love again

The mothers death

Hand over ear

It will be ok
It will be ok
It will be ok
It will be ok

Mom I feel you
Can't see you

<u>Benj 8:48 am 4/24/16</u>

A Girl

A girl
Whose heart is the rose of time
A girl
Shyness of a woman's grace
A girl
Their radiance of love
A girl
Mothers of time
Grace thee
A girl
Brings angels to smile
A girl
Eyes that twinkle
As stars so bright
A girl
Her presence is of swooping flower
The sweet smells
A girl
Warmeth thy heart
Oh, heavens above!
For this girl
Is a creation of you
Magnificent

Benj 2:30 pm 2/14/15

Christ of Mine

Christ of mine
Creator of thine
For the wishes of thee
Upon the worlds
Blood of life

Surround thee with hope
Of the breaths and the wind
And the crown of glory
For a younger man's heart
Has forever changed

For the wood of nails
The chest of blood
The ankles of iron
The shroud of thorns
The walk
Grace of pain
The agony of the world's pain

The time is the same as it is in the past
For man's wickedness of fear
Of a man who teaches:

Open up the heavens
And I shall find you
Look up into the clouds
The brilliance, of the sun's rays

As it sneaks through and forever warms your face
For the story's still told today as it was yesterday
Man dies, man is born,
And still there is mystery of who we are

But beyond the years of years
And the forward of life . . . it still doesn't change
Life is just a brief salt . . . that's flickered
within the wind of the pouring rain
That disappears and appears

Life is short
Comfort thee
Run
A cloud of . . . Beautiful sunshine
That warms a man's heart

For I know, Lord, you are there
The fear of existence, the fear of the unknown
But we cry out as fear overwhelms us
And life is fleeting
And those who believe . . . Cry out . . .
Cry out . . .
Cry out . . .
For they know the peace, for they have peace

**This poem is written for my sister-in-law Rose and my niece Kelly.
I wrote this poem while I held the cross you game me on my birthday.
I closed my eyes and held onto it and spoke these very words you just heard.
I Love you, guys . . .
<u>Benj</u>**

The Clouds of Angels

Oh lord I stoop to thee-
I plead for her mercy
The love of a stone
An important drop of love
i plead o' lord to her-
I plead oh lord of your love
Squeeze drops of lemon to heal my cuts-
My pain of loneliness
Suffering to exist without love
Rest on my pillow- beside the dreams of fear, pride, and hurt-
Oh how I miss her
The pit of a well screaming, screaming!
Love me- love me-!
Oh voices of myself be gone-
Let me soar on the wings of my angels.

Benj 8:55 am 5/20/15

Is It You

Is it you
I've cried so many times
Waiting for you
Is it you
I have searched the depths of my soul
Yearning for you
Is it you
I've waited and waited
You passing by
Through my life, wondering
Is it you
The lonely nights
The four corners of my room, wondering
Is it you
My heart yearns for you desperately
Screaming out
Is it you
Yes, love, it's me
I'm here,
Opens arms
Come to me—I'll love you

<u>Benj 6:00 am 3/27/09</u>

L

A girl
Loneliness comes beyond the trees of the past

Fill this hole of emptiness

Yearning, searching a baby's cry

The year's fly by, eyes wide open

Holding the tears as I crawl, as I walk as I run!

Beyond the fear of being touched, longing to be held

Scared, scared, life of love
Moments of hope

Clinging for they don't know of my wanting, in my mind

Only to reach, hands stretched out

Holding of hands
Joy explodes -screaming-
Little boy dancing-
Smiling!!!!!

Missing her all my life
She appeared briefly
Beyond the search

Hope of her eyes staring
In my eyes -dancing children

Slowly our hands are apart
Gobbled up in the fears of life

We cry silently

I love you so L
Still love you!!!!

<u>Benj 9:25 pm 2/19/16</u>

Why Love

Why love

How I miss you
The pain is so deep
But-

Why love

Days and days all I see-
There can be a distract
Of time,
But-

Why love

For told of birth
All living things,
Feed on love and in desperate need of love
But -

Why love

It's in you my child
Hands stretched out,
Needing, waiting for you
But-

Why love

Since time I forgive,
Love for its pain emptiness
But-

Why love

Stranded, desolate

No water, thirsty of
A glance in her eyes;
Will you love me?
But-

Why love

Yearning of her hands
Deeply crying
Missing the love of her eyes
But-

Why love

The crying inside
When quiet come-
The emptiness
Screaming!

Why love

Why love - Why love
Why -
My child you are loved
I love you, put your head on my shoulder, let me comfort your tears, let me embrace you and squeeze all the pain out,
And fill you with love

Yes Love

Yes Love
Yes- Yes- Yes
Reach to me again!!

<u>Benj 9:43 3/6/2016</u>

My True Self

My true self
Fulfilled in a body of love

My true self
Feels the deepness of love

My true self
Connects with souls

My true self
Feels the joy and pain of others

My true self
Loves to love

My true self
A smile, a glance,

To bring your heart,
And your soul joy and love,
Through the window of eyes passing by

Amen lord I pray

<u>**Benj 7:30 pm 2/16/16**</u>

Full-Sized Render

Let the grace of time be ever at your side
Let the wings of men be strong with you
Let life embrace your journey—
Angels follow above
And surround you
Your heart is a gold cup
That is filled with compassion

Benj 10:36 am 2/27/15

Kristel Heart

A girl
Whose heart is the pure beauty of a glowing moon

The brightness of her soul
Reaches deep in the eyes of many

Her smile is of love

Her eyes twinkle with joy
Of comfort

Saying I see u, I love u
I may not know u-
But I get you

Love me and I'll love you-
And be your friend

My beauty is not skin deep
But it travels the world of love

See me-see me-my heart
My soul, my love

For you are the woman of time
Who breathes life into the world around you
So see me, I am love
Filled with love So just love me!

Benj 9:25 pm 2/19/16

The Lift

The little girl within you- so protected
I see you, your hurt; your pain
Cometh let it out,
Your pain- don't zip it up-
For your love is buried in you-running scared!!
Quiet my child
Your heart is pure
It has always been pure-
Evil comes and scares you, so you have hurt my little boy
Protected always
In fear-
For you have been damaged and afflicted by your father
I oust thee!
Our hearts together are the children of
innocence; reach for each other,
Hold my hand
In the graces of Heaven
Purifies protection from the angels
Please soothe my heart
For the devils anger hurts and pain whispers in my ear-
Peace, peace-
My lord I bow to you
I let go-
I let go of my ego, lord-
It travels along men's mysteries of time
For the mother of love eludes them
I bow and kneel,
Forgive me-wrap me with angels
You comfort me and love me

Benj 5:22 pm 11/4/15

Kindness upon Thee

For the foul mouth
The stench is tasted for days
For the memory of time lost—
For we have one life
Wait not another day

Forces of blind men will help you see—
Beyond your own blindness, of ego and fears
To release this love, let it be sprayed upon this world

There is no ego among the masses
Forever giving of one's self,
Oh, I eat of the fruit of love
Coming from your heart,
Your heart runs red
With apples and sweetness

Benj 10:45 pm 2/13/15

Forgiveness

Forgiveness, forgiveness

Hold the lonely
Take the mask off
Let us cry together

Purity of love
Our eyes tell the story
of our soul

Look at each other
Deep we follow a familiar path

Forgiveness, forgiveness

Our hands stretched out
Reach for the heavens
of love

Take the burdens
Of thy ego of self
Look, look in our eyes
Hi, hi -how are you

Two hearts beat the same vein
Filled with blood
Yearning for acceptance

Hi, I see you as I look in your eyes
I scream with eyes
I feel you pain
I feel you love

Look, look - look

My eyes travel deep in the depths of you

I breath and take you in
Heavens of pure light
Gods melt love on us

And you are not alone

Look, look

Scream out with joy as we dance
As smiles spread across our faces

Hi- Hi, for this split second of gaze
I am holding you as the Angels cuddle with us

This emptiness!
Fill it oh god! Oh old Angels!
Weeping with love and joy
Out stretch your wings and engulf us

Breath my child, I am god's angel here to love and protect you
Breath me in
I'm always here
Cry your minds eye, your hope, your dreams
O'lord release us in your glow of purity

Let us rest and float in this warmth of
a radiant white glorious light

Amen

Benj 8:53 pm 4/17/16

Loneliness

Loneliness comes beyond the trees of the past

Fill this hole of emptiness
Yearning this hole of emptiness
Yearning, searching, a baby's cry

The year's fly by-
Eyes wide open

Holding the tears as I crawl, as I walk, as I run
Beyond the fear of being touched, longing to be held

Scared, Scared, of this life of love-

Moments of hope, clinging!
For they don't know of the wanting in my mind

Only to reach with hands stretched out

Holding of hands-

Joy explodes -screaming!
Little boy dancing-
Smiling!!!!!

Missing her all my life
She appeared briefly
Beyond the search

Hope in her eyes
Staring in my eyes
Dancing children

Slowly our hands are apart,
Gobbled up in the fears of life

We cry silently

I love you so - L
Still I love you!!!!

<u>Benj 8:30 pm 2/16/16</u>

CPSIA information can be obtained
at www.ICGtesting.com
Printed in the USA
LVHW040256060623
748787LV00002B/385